EAST INDIA COMPANY SHIPS AT DEPTFORD

Anonymous, British School, C. 1683, National Maritime Museum, London, Greenwich.

INVOLVED WITH MANKIND

INVOLVED WITH MANKIND

A THEOLOGY OF CHAPLAINCY

MICHAEL A. MILTON, PHD

BETHESDA
PUBLISHING GROUP

Copyright © 2023 by Michael A. Milton, PhD and Bethesda Publishing Group, a division of Faith for Living, Inc., a 501c3 North Carolina nonprofit corporation.

All rights reserved.

The PRCC: Presbyterian and Reformed Commission on Chaplains and Military Personnel is authorized for unlimited use in all media.

All others:

No part of this book may be reproduced in any form or by any electronic or mechanical means, including information storage and retrieval systems, without written permission from the author, except for the use of brief quotations in a book review.

For the glory of God and to Bible-believing Chaplains who fight the good fight of faith each day. Always for my wife.

No man is an island, entire of itself; every man is a piece of the continent, a part of the main. If a clod be washed away by the sea, Europe is the less, as well as if a promontory were, as well as if a manor of thy friend's or of thine own were: any man's death diminishes me, because I am involved in mankind, and therefore never send to know for whom the bells tolls; it tolls for thee.

John Donne, *Devotions Upon Emergent Occasions*, "Meditation XVII"

CONTENTS

FOREWORD

This monograph is the first in a series on a theology of chaplaincy. Commissioned by Dr. Jim Carter, Executive Director of the PRCC, I came to this project with great excitement. I have served as a chaplain, pastor, church planter, and as both a senior administrator and a tenured professor in theological higher education. I have often thought about the theological issues involved with chaplaincy. I have, also, considered the misunderstandings that can sometimes cause those in parish ministry to ask questions about the validity of word and sacrament ministry in a secular setting. Conversely, chaplains have not always communicated their case for the justification of chaplaincy. Both parties are usually over-worked and don't have time to pursue these questions. I wrote this with a prayer that the Church will be convinced that not only is chaplain ministry a vital genre of the ministry of word and sacrament, but that it is needed more now than ever. Ever sector of chaplaincy—e.g.,healthcare, workplace, first responders, correctional, sports, airport, and Armed Forces—is experiencing growth just as similar studies show other ministries of the Church in decline. How is that? That is just one of the issues we will examine in this theology of chaplaincy. I pray it will be of benefit and blessing to you and a support, in some small way, to the advance of the Gospel of Jesus Christ in our generation.

Michael A. Milton, PhD
Sunday before Pentecost 2023

1

WHY A THEOLOGY OF CHAPLAINCY IS NEEDED
EMPIRICAL AND ANECDOTAL EVIDENCE AND DISCUSSION

Chaplaincy is a distinct Gospel ministry expression of the historic ordained pastoral ministry, viz., ministers of Word and Sacrament. This assertion is not without detractors, most of whom are fellow ministers who continue to understand the nature of ordained ministry as related to a place, i.e., a local congregation. Ecclesiology is, then, subject to being interpreted through the lens of parochial structures rather than the mission of the Church in the world. We do not dismiss the primacy of settled Christian communities. We merely advocate for "recognizing the integrity of chaplaincy as a genre of ministry and its significance within the mission of the wider Church."[1] However, the response of some may be to practically treat the chaplaincy as an anomaly within ministry rather than a strategic and historical expression of pastoral ministry. This monograph addresses this tension by considering a theology of chaplaincy from Scripture and in practice. Firstly, however, we want to establish why such a paper is needed.

Chaplaincy Growth is a Phenomenon to Explore

Chaplain ministry is growing even as church attendance is declining.[2] This fact calls us, the Church, to ask why and to consider its meaning for the broader work of the Church. Consider theological higher education (a facet of church life that has occupied many decades of my life). The phenomenon of chaplain growth amid the decline of other programs is reflected in theological seminaries. This is so within Presbyterian and Reformed churches as it is in different traditions in Christianity. As local pastors are increasingly burning out and dropping out

(42% admit they are "burned out" and preparing to leave the ministry, and only one in ten will retire as a pastor as of 2022), chaplaincy is on the rise.[3] Statistician Chris Meinzer the most recent findings (2023) to constituency schools of ATS: "So, across ATS schools, MDiv enrollment is declining."[4] The Master of Divinity degree, the North American standard degree for ordained ministry, as of 2023, is no longer the reason people go to seminary. Indeed, the MDiv is, for the first time in ATS history, second to Master of Arts degrees (see Figure 1). The trend to replace the Master of Divinity with a Master of Arts has been coming. We have studied the trends for more than a decade. The MA, now, appears to be the future.[5]

However, as theological higher education continues to experience a steady decline, chaplain programs within seminaries are one of the only areas of growth: "In the context of well-documented declines in theological school enrollments, specialized education for chaplaincy appears to be an area of growth. Of the 270 Association of Theological Schools (ATS) member schools, candidates, and affiliates, just under 70 offer some type of specialized chaplaincy program."[6] Moreover, theological seminaries are creating partnerships with agencies offering Clinical Pastoral Education (CPE). The author was involved with bringing the Institute of Clinical Pastoral Training (ICPT) to Presbyterian and Reformed Chaplaincy training as an evangelical alternative to older ACPE programs. The ICPT is now breaking new records in enrollment. The popularity of chaplain ministries is, naturally, of interest to the Association of Theological Schools. Indeed, ATS awarded its most prestigious grant to design a center for chaplain studies at one of its constituent schools. The justification for their support is understandable: "Professional chaplaincy is a growing area within the practice of ministry. Chaplaincy is also a dynamic vocation within a variety of settings including but not limited to hospitals, higher education, retirement communities, military institutions, correctional settings, law enforcement, fire protection, and emergency response organizations." In other words, in a day when theological education is searching for a positive storyline, the chaplaincy is the undeniable place to look:

Attention to chaplaincy and spiritual care in theological education is growing, particularly since 2000. In addition to offering single classes, a quarter of the theological schools we identified have degree programs that address chaplaincy, and that number seems to still be on the rise. From MDiv programs to MA programs to a few DMin and PhD programs that focus on chaplaincy in the military, health care, or more broadly, chaplaincy seems to be one of few growth areas in theological education today.[7]

These partnerships can not only allow for an apprenticeship model of training to wed with the academic model of theological education but also can provide academic credit hours for CPE. Preparing Gospel ministers by academic education with vocational training is not only the most effective and efficient method but is the norm in church history. The North American adaptation of the professional model of graduate education is an anomaly in the Church and in church history.[8] From the catechetical school of Alexander to the present situation in the Anglican Church in Uganda, the ordinary method of preparing the next generation of pastors and, teachers, evangelists, some of whom would become doctors of the Church, includes the rigorous academic and devotional study of the Bible and its interpretation, and those studies that are necessary to advance the former, viz., rhetoric and logic, history, comparative religion, literature, philosophy, and human (i.e., social) studies.

Interest in clinical pastoral education (CPE) is also growing. Between 2005 and 2015, the number of student units of CPE completed increased by 25% . . . Although most CPE centers are not affiliated with theological schools, growing numbers are—since 2002, 12 theological schools in the United States have established their own CPE centers or started hosting satellite centers.[9]

There are successful models of these centers in North America, the UK, and in Europe. The UK models provide an educational and training model for chaplaincy (and the ministry) that combines the trends we are now seeing in American seminaries: academic study via a Master of Arts and vocational training through, e.g., a chaplain center. Three of the best-known centers of influence are The Cardiff Centre for Chaplaincy Studies, The Oxford Centre for Ecclesiology & Practical Theology (affiliated with the Church of England), and the Gerald E. Marsh Center for Chaplain Studies (an unaffiliated center in the Baptist tradition located at B. H. Carroll Theological Seminary, Irving, Texas).[10] Regrettably, our Presbyterian and Reformed seminaries are not leading in this area. Of the typical seminaries producing chaplains for the PRCC endorsing agency, only one (as of this writing), Erskine Theological Seminary, has a Master of Divinity in Chaplain Ministries degree program (requiring CPE training with the academic curriculum).[11] The lack of attention among seminaries in the Reformed tradition is baffling, given the history of Calvinist involvement with chaplaincy. Moreover, the Kuyperian (Abraham Kuyper, 1837-1920) theological strain that continues in at least part of the PRCC churches would undoubtedly welcome the robust transformational approach to Church and the World. Kuyper believed Calvinism was a "life system" that should be applied to every segment of human endeavor.[12] Chaplaincy is (regardless of one's theological commitments or identity) an essentially Kuyperian undertaking.[13] Niebuhr's *Christ and Culture* is helpful at this point.[14] Niebuhr's five possible responses of Christians to culture are: Christ against culture, Christ of culture, Christ above culture, Christ and culture in paradox, and *Christ the transformer of culture*. The Calvinistic view, grounded in Christ's command to be salt and light (Matthew 5:13-16), and His call for us to go into the world (Matthew 28:19-20) to love our enemies, and pray for those who despise for Christ's sake (Matthew 5:44), remembering that such were some of us (1 Corinthians 6:1) before God's rich mercy (Ephesians 2:4) brought about a new birth, is, clearly, to approach the world in expectation of *transformation* (John 4:35). For the syllogisms of this world are exploded before the glorious God and Father of our Lord Jesus Christ. This transformation is the positive product of unconditional election, and irresistible grace. Herein is the glorious ground where our chaplains stand. Thus, rejecting a dualistic conception of God's creation, embracing a biblical-theological vision for ministry, and knowing the times, our PRCC chaplains enter the hospitals, Armed Forces, prisons, corporations, airports, and other institutions with Gospel expectation.

Indeed, chaplaincy continues to grow and expand in North America. It is one of the only bright spots in the reporting of the Association of Theological Schools (see Figure 2). This is not only so in English-speaking countries. European nations also report an increase in chaplains.[15] One example is Norway, where the growth is producing a new harvest of research for the field. Another example is Denmark. Denmark may be one of the most secular nations on earth, yet church attendance declines chaplain ministry is rising dramatically.[16] Why the disparity between the vocational enthusiasm of parish ministers and chaplains? More work is needed. However, it appears that the "secular age" has a significant part to play. As Western peoples become more secularized, parish ministry declines. Yet the human spirit is unrelenting in its need for spiritual guidance. The nature of chaplaincy also contributes to its popularity. Chaplains minister in areas that are not driven by organizational issues necessarily faced by their parish pastoral colleagues. As one Methodist minister told the author, "I am leaving parish ministry to become a military chaplain. I am asking for deployment to a battle zone." When questioned about leaving a bustling suburban congregation for a battlefield, the minister replied, "It is really simple. If I am to be shot, I prefer to know who the enemy is, and that they use real bullets." It was an unforgettable reply that seemed to encapsulate the modern crisis in parish-based pastoral ministry.[17] The turbulent worship wars, false expectations of pastors as CEOs rather than shepherds (by both seminary graduates and congregations), megachurches viewed as a positive model to be followed, liturgy in the age of show-business, and mounting tensions over a loss of significance in the community, have contributed to the present malaise. Alternatively, the chaplain ministry is growing in all sectors (e.g., Armed Forces, healthcare, corporate, corrections, sports, palliative care, and first responders). The data is consistent for both parish ministry decline and chaplaincy growth, on a macro level and in the Presbyterian and Reformed Commission on Chaplains (the endorsing agency and chaplain ministry for a covenanted association of like-minded conservative and evangelical Presbyterian denominations and patron for this monograph).[18] The chaplain faces equally difficult challenges as his parish minister counterpart. Working with human beings and applying the truth of God's word with pastoral wisdom is challenging in any facet of ministry. However, the chaplain enjoys a work environment where chaplains are often valued, sought out, and esteemed as valuable members of the larger team. The statistics for the state of affairs in parish-based ministry are all too well known.

Thus, could chaplaincy growth be associated with the rise of secularism? The qualitative research suggests a positive correlation. Is chaplaincy growth a flowering of Calvinism, an ascendancy of a theological method that transcends denominationalism, and offers a comprehensive worldview that is portable, relatable, and compelling in even the most pluralistic environments? As we will see later in this monograph Calvinism is one of the most theologically and practically fertile incubators of chaplain ministry. The "life-system" of Calvinism (which we argue is the system of relationships taught in Scripture) has demonstrated its ability to thrive and expand in otherwise difficult philosophical times. Since Calvinism adheres to a biblical interpretation that presupposes a knowledge of God, this genre of ministry is particularly suited to thrive in theological plurality. We believe that the rise of the secular age and the post secular age (and we anticipate Habermas' "post-secularism" will not hinder but continue the interest and subsequent growth of chaplaincy) has provided an open door for chaplain ministry in the Western nations.[19] Concerning the relationship of the chaplaincy to parish ministry we can ask other questions. Does the locus of chaplaincy within the institutions of the secular age create a built-in suspicion of confessional fidelity by those in parish pastoral ministry? Could the perceived tension between parish-based ministry, including missions to establish parish-based ministries, and chaplain ministry, be located in the missional incongruities between the two?[20] For the German scholar, Jürgen Habermas (b. 1929), a Christian, postmodernity and "the secularization hypothesis has now lost its explanatory power and that religion and the secular world always stand in a reciprocal relation."[21] Post-secularism is, thus, a reaction to the absence of a religious component in dialogical pre-supposition. While not embracing a Judeo-Christian theism or even welcoming its contributions, post-secularism must inevitably come to recognize the limits of secularism and the certain failure of postmodernity's "theater of the absurd."[22] Thus, Habermas's assessment: "Among the modern societies, only those that are able to introduce into the secular domain the essential contents of their religious traditions which point beyond the mere human realm will also be able to rescue the substance of the human."[23] The shifting philosophical winds have caused writers like Hunter and Volf to consider Christian responses to post-secularism. Hunter urges believers to adapt Jeremiah 29:7 as the ruling motif of witness in the secular and post secular ages ("But seek the welfare of the city where I have sent you into exile, and pray to the LORD on its behalf, for in its welfare you will find your welfare" ESV). He calls the response a "faithful presence."[24] For Volf, "The prophetic role of Christian communities — their engagement to mend the world, to foster human flourishing, and to serve the common good—is nothing but their identity projecting itself outward in word and deed."[25] As a former instructor and writer for the Army's Chaplain Center and School at Fort Jackson, SC, the strategies are amazingly similar to our guidance to newly commissioned Chaplains.

Summary

Chaplaincy is a growing ministry genre. However, its ascendancy occurs as parish ministry is declining. If there were no other presenting issues than chaplain ministry growth in a time of general religious decline that would be significant enough for investigating a theology of chaplaincy. However, there are other variables in play. One of those is the nature of the relationship between chaplains and parish ministry. The former facts alone suggest the likelihood of some level of tension. Beyond plausible competitiveness, are there other possible explanations for the distance between parish ministry and chaplaincy? One answer is, "Yes, the very nature of the two is so different that it appears incongruous." Parish ministry and chaplaincy are not inharmonious. However, significant distinctions should be addressed if deeper mutual understanding is to be found.

Distinctions of Chaplaincy and Parish Ministry

The nature of the chaplaincy inevitably raises the question of fidelity concerning the minister who conducts such ministry. Such is understandable given the human proclivity for classifying life into *le sacré et le profane.*

The Sacred and the Profane

The chaplaincy operates in the arena of "the profane." Émile Durkheim, the brilliant but agnostic French Jew sometimes mentioned as a founding father of sociology, wrote extensively on the idea of the "sacred and the profane."[26] In *The Elementary Forms of Religious Life (1912)*, his final work, Durkheim rightly observed religion as the most fundamental association in human societies. Yet, as Durkheim defined religious identity by its common conviction of what is holy, i.e., sacred, the great Sociologist—we believe, mistakenly—proposed that the sacred is also shaped by what is profane. This dualism might be observed when the articles of a respective religion confess its faith within a meritocratic framework. Thus, to put it simply, the more sacred things in one's life and the fewer profane things create a tally that leans toward an earned righteousness. That Émile Durkheim should arrive at this conclusion when observing world religions (as he did most convincingly in his study) is neither mistaken nor overstated. However, it is incomplete. While such an attitude of sacred/secular as a division with religious benefits to the human soul may be observed in some Christians and in some people identifying as Christian, we know that no such dualism exists or could exist in the true faith taught by our Lord Jesus Christ. Such dualism is, in fact, one reason that the Jewish rabbinate grew increasingly hostile. For the Lord Jesus ate and drank with sinners (Matthew 9:10-17, Mark 2:15-22, Luke 5:29-39). The Lord re-interpreted His own Word away from the captivity of the scribes when, for example, He taught in Mark 2:27, "The Sabbath was made for man, not man for the Sabbath." In his paper on "Holy Time and Sacred Space in Puritan New England," James Walsh summarized the understanding of this remarkable Reformed community: "To a Christian, no time or place could ever be more appropriate for prayer than another."[27] Yet, Reformed Christianity did not reject the reality of space and time and its meaning to the believer. Consider the scholarly treatment of the matter by Douglas Davies: "The idea of a heavenly Jerusalem in Christian thought offers a dramatic example of the way an actual place comes to function symbolically as an expression of faith and hope."[28] Moreover, "In theological terms sacred places are special because they speak of the power and grace of God that was evident in the lives of past believers."[29] Yet, in no way does visiting, for example, the tomb of Charles Haddon Spurgeon (1834-1892) at Norwood Cemetery, in the London Burrough of Lambeth, pausing to contemplate his life and God's power demonstrated, equate to the applied theology of one who assigns "holiness" to one material object and not another.[30] Nevertheless, the fact remains, that Reformed Christianity following on Scripture that values certain historical sites for their illustrative benefits—a contribution to sanctification by virtue of their aid to memory, and memory of the acts of God in the world—but in no way supports a construction of sacred and profane, i.e., sacred and secular. The chaplain's ministry to Exxon or to the NYPD is not diminished by their respective organizational mission statements. That such work is more difficult, more isolated, more in need of the wisdom to navigate the intricate human organizational labyrinths that emerge at the intersection of Gospel ministry and commerce may be posited without need of citation. That Gospel ministry is valid whether the stipendiary role is paid by an organized community of believers or an enterprise that operates "outside of the gates." The British Methodist Church was thoroughly Reformed at this very point:

The gospels describe the ministry of Jesus, very largely outside of and, to some extent, away from the places of gathered worship – synagogue and temple.4 Jesus conducts his ministry in homes or in the open air, in the places where people live and work, and this was very largely outside the confines of the gathered faith community.

This is a serious challenge to the Church which instinctively looks inwards and is concerned with its own preservation. Our calling as disciples is to live out the meaning and the message of the gospel in word and deed. It is to make real in our own time and place, the ministry of Jesus.[31]

Philosophical dualism—assigning virtue to spirit over matter—or practical dualism—assigning merit to one place over another—is the antithesis of Reformed thought grounded in Scripture.[32] Indeed, the Scriptures are clear: "He has made everything beautiful in its time. Also, he has put eternity into man's heart, yet so that he cannot find out what God has done from the beginning to the end" (Ecclesiastes 3:11), and; "For everything created by God is good, and nothing is to be rejected if it is received with thanksgiving" (1 Timothy 4:4). Yet, those in the Reformed faith are as subject to the default position of practical dualism. Practical dualism denies that there is spiritual merit to be gained by place while erecting a working (not confessional) ecclesiology that adopts the concept of secular and sacred. An unintended but real dualistic mindset considers the work of, e.g., a corporate chaplain bringing Christian witness to an oil company engaged in offshore drilling activities as something different than a missionary. If the chaplain is employed by the oil company (though as a chaplain with no restrictions on his convictions) and bears witness to Christ among those who either deny Him or ignore Him we might think, "His ordination vows and confessional integrity are at risk. There is no local church, no formalized mission. He is flying solo over the flames." Of course, such a response is true to a point. The corporate chaplain in our example is, indeed, "at risk." He might be the only believer aboard that rig in the Gulf. There is no local church or missionary team to support him. He is "flying solo" in the sense that he bears witness to the Savior (and the Reformed faith) in a most precarious position. So, one might add, "The chaplain is, then, ministering sacred things amid the profane" And this is the point of departure from Calvinism. The theology that arose from the Reformation, which was a revival of the teachings of Scripture and the interpretation by the early church fathers, saw no distinction between sacred and profane (in the sense of a supposed merit gained). As Jesus sent the disciples out, as He called Saul of Tarsus, so He continues to call men to proclaim the unsearchable riches of Christ beyond the boundaries of "Jerusalem." Christian communities should be established as ordinary means to fulfill the great commission of Jesus Christ. Building up local churches is vital to the faith. The local church remains predominant in the work of fulfilling the Great Commission. However, the extraordinary does not negate the ordinary but enlarges its ministry. This infiltration of the institutions and ideological realms that are otherwise apathetic or antagonistic toward the gospel of Jesus Christ is a legitimate extension of the Church to the world. Dangerous? Undoubtedly so. Risky? Always. Isolated? Of course. A legitimate ministry of Word and Sacrament? Absolutely.

But how does the extraordinary ministry of the chaplaincy in the ordinary expression of ministry in the parish locate points of understanding? One way is to examine the distinctive features of the incongruity. In doing so, it is possible to imagine that the paradox of the gospel presents in chaplain ministry (the Church in the world, Christ among the antagonists) becomes a recognizable point of theological commonality. The following represents only a few touch points that might bring greater understanding. So, we could put it like this: "What are the differences in the functions of parish-based ministry and chaplain ministry?" These variables are vital to consider for they touch on the heart of a theology of chaplaincy as it relates to ecclesiology.

Communities served.

Parish-based ministry is defined by its relationship to the Christian community. Chaplain ministry is defined by its relationship with people in other communities. Beyond ordination and reception by the local adjudicatory, i.e., the presbytery, the entrance to conduct the Gospel ministry of Word and Sacrament is quite different for one to be pastor and the other to be chaplain. The pastor is received by congregational approbation. The chaplain is received by the official organs of employment like any other employee or member of the institution (e.g., commissioning in the Armed Forces, a hiring protocol for respective state and federal correctional institutions). The respective centers of influence for the minister serving as a pastor in a civilian Christian community as well as the minister serving as a chaplain are the official organs of governance and administration. However, those authorities differ significantly. The chaplain reports to a superior who may or may not be a minister of the Gospel. The parish minister is bound, according to denominational ecclesiology, to a local assembly of representative "governors," e.g., a session. Therefore, the dynamics of ministry are different. While both are in a matrix in which peers (church or employer) make policy and pastors/chaplains carry out policy the similarities tend to end there.

Boundaries of Belief

Parish-based ministry exercises word and sacrament pastoral ministry to believers (mostly) in confessional agreement. Chaplain ministry exercises word and sacrament pastoral ministry in the context of secular communities. This does not mean that the sacraments are administered to unbelievers. On the contrary, as Christian communities are identified and assembled, or as a body of believers is established within the borders of unbelief, the chaplain acting as an evangelist (in Presbyterianism, the powers of an evangelist are granted and guarded by the jurisdiction of presbyters, viz., the presbytery, or the highest court appointing a commission, like the PRCC, to oversee the discharge of the evangelist office and duties to a respective minister) in conducting services on the

Lord's Day and other days, including preaching, administration of baptism and the Lord's Supper. Without fear of hyperbole, it may be said that the PRCC chaplain is under the watchful eye of other presbyters more than many overseas missionaries. To wit, all necessary resources are deployed to ensure that the chaplain remains faithful to the respective ordination vows, and able to freely conduct ministry within a highly pluralist setting that might otherwise be insulated from the Gospel. No ecclesiastical stretching is needed to justify the chaplain as minister of Word and Sacrament. Historic, traditional Reformed polity (British and Continental) rests on a ministry conducted under the jurisdiction of plural governance likewise comprised of individuals appointed by representative, plural governance.[33]

Cultural Contexts

Parish-based ministry is expressed within the context of Christian culture. Chaplain ministry is conducted within the context of worldly cultures. As any culture or organizational behavior student knows, distinctions and differences, compared and contrasted, can lead to understanding or to mistrust and even division. The case with parish ministers and chaplains is heightened by the fact that chaplains of a respective denomination spend more time with chaplains of other denominations than with their own.

Community Commitments

Parish-based ministry is supported by its own worldview in the Christian community. Chaplain base ministry expresses a Christian worldview in the context of competing worldviews. While most chaplains find the opportunity to proclaim Christ amid such diversity a vocationally satisfying part of the mission, others outside of chaplaincy might look at the situation differently. Some might be tempted to compare the scenario to foreign missionaries. Yet, the comparison is notably different for at least one remarkable reason: foreign missionaries are not paid by those they seek to evangelize. Those concerned about erosion of faith in chaplain ministries are right to draw out this distinction. This high degree of tangible affinity with a secular organization disrupts a desire to support the chaplain from, e.g., parish ministers. What are we to make of this? I believe the answer lies in the area of wisdom and the example of tentmaking.

If the Church could cause unbelievers to finance the mission of the Church without demanding usury in the form of compromise of the Gospel, we might proceed with caution yet proceed, nevertheless. The truth is that employers (whether a municipality-supported first responder or the United States Air Force) that are also the chaplain's designated "people group" value something the chaplain brings to the table. That value is often attached to the overall well-being of employees. This value is not a guess but the result of research with human resource managers about the role of chaplains in the workplace. The title of one such research project summarizes the value attached to companies hiring chaplains very well: "The 'suits' care about us."[34]

The other factor in play is tentmaking.[35] Luke wrote about Paul's trade in Acts 18:3, "and because he was of the same trade, he stayed with them and worked, for they were tentmakers by trade." Mission by tentmaking is an often-overlooked *norm* that exists in Christian missions. The prophet Amos of Tekoa (under Jeroboam II, 793-753, and Uzziah) was a herdsman and shepherd and engaged with the commercial preparation of farmer of the red fig variety *Ficus sycomorus L.*[36] "Then Amos answered and said to Amaziah, 'I was no prophet, nor a prophet's son, but I was a herdsman and a dresser of sycamore figs. But the Lord took me from following the flock, and the Lord said to me, "Go, prophesy to my people Israel"'" (Amos 7:14-15, ESV). In a scholarly publication, James Francis and Leslie Francis make the case that tentmaking remains a compelling strategy for Christian missions in the twenty-first century.[37] The concern over pay is embedded in the description of the strategy, "tentmaking," and, thus, the issue of non-stipendiary ministry is unavoidable. Besides the efficiency of such a strategy, tentmaking is theologically compelling. The tentmaker is identifying with those being reached with the Gospel. This incarnational facet of the mission is Christologically satisfying in its presentation of ministry. The chaplain is a tentmaker with an ostensible *raison d'être:* the chaplain supports the organizational mission by strengthening the spirits of those in the organization. This is not a Trojan horse scheme but rather a legitimate strategy for reaching others through the theological method of incarnation.

Tribal Tongue

Parish-based ministry speaks in the language of the Christian faith. Chaplain ministry must maintain the language of the Christian faith while learning to express the Christian faith in the native language of the host institution.

Locus *Stare*

The Latin *locus stare* means "a place to stand." *The locus stare* is not merely a geographic point, the location. Rather, the *locus stare* is the environment in which one conducts ministry. The *locus stare* for a Christian shepherd serving as a parish minister is strikingly dissimilar to the *locus stare* of a chaplain. For the former the "place to stand" is a community of like-minded theological commitment. For the latter the *locus stare* is a community linked by like-minded institutional purpose. The difference is significant in at least two crucial ways affecting ministry. Firstly, a local church is, ordinarily, a place where the pastor's faith is supported. However, a correctional institution, for example, is not organized by allegiance to any one religion but exists for institutional purpose. The chaplain posted in San Quentin State Prison speaks the Gospel in an essentially unsupported "place to stand." This is not to say that the chaplain is unwelcome. Nor does it presuppose opposition to his message. In other words, a pastor conducts ministry within a society of people gathered out of common faith. The locus stare means the chaplain is not announcing the Gospel in a community gathered for a religious purpose. Their organizational relationship is defined by their association to San Quentin, whether as an inmate, an employee, or even a volunteer. The implications of *locus stare* are manifold. Therefore, secondly, the chaplain's relationship to others in the community is ostensibly grounded in organizational commitment (or *commital* in the case of prisoners). Thirdly, this dissimilarity of locus stare can create misunderstanding or even suspicion between a parish minister The Parish-based ministry can and should promote prophetic preaching to the community at large. However, the message is often given from within the Christian community. Chaplain ministry orders the prophetic message of Christ within the camp of those who often deny him.

Homogeneity versus Plurality

Parish-based ministry is supported by the Christian community. Chaplain base ministry is most often supported by the institution they serve. There is a remarkable irony in this feature chaplain ministry. Often, the institution is highly pluralistic and resistant (at times even antagonistic) to the exclusive claims of the Lord Jesus Christ. Nevertheless, the institution values the evidence-based merits — efficiencies and effectiveness — that a Christian minister brings to the institutional community.

Organizational Tensions

Parish ministry is conducted mostly without the tension of unbelief. Division in the local church occurs when there are competing visions of the particular tradition within the Christian faith or disagreement on operation strategies and tactics. Tensions in the chaplain ministry do not ordinarily arise from other believers in the institutional community served but rather from those who wish to see the Christian witness silenced, neutered, or removed altogether. Thus, we may state (not without some overlap of the two conditions): While the pastor of a local church must invariably endure the slings and arrows of fellow believers, the chaplain must face the opposition to his very presence as a witness to Jesus Christ.

Summary

The present situation is abundantly clear: while theological higher education is undergoing remarkable change, with outcomes uncertain, and the dropout rate of pastors continues to climb, chaplaincy, as a distinct ministry genre, is experiencing unprecedented growth. The reasons for this growth appear to coincide with the secularization of Western society. We might also opine that the continuing challenges of parish ministry in a secular age have some bearing on the growth of chaplaincy. As there are more churches being closed than planted, with more congregations losing membership than gaining, we are witnesses to a veritable evacuation route from the local church (this is to be mourned; yet, happily, there are examples of churches, including PRCC-related congregations bucking the trends). It is as if we are looking upon a grainy black-and-white film from WWII in Europe: broken ministers and families, lay leaders and disillusioned parishioners pulling old wooden carts packed with former Christian book bestsellers on church growth, walking weary and war-torn by failed liturgical innovations, and outreach campaigns. Mercifully, the salve of Scripture and the Spirit of God will ameliorate wounds from the entanglement with Postmodernity. As these refugees from the worship wars, and the organizational behavior studies, seek shelter from the Secular

Age, the chaplaincy moves deeper beyond the boundaries of belief. It is as if chaplaincy was made for secularism. For chaplaincy shines in even the most pluralistic or antagonistic environments. As long as the chaplain is true to his faith and endorsing agency confessional statements, and the host sees value in his presence, he can minister faithfully beyond the institutional parish church system. These seven factors that distinguish chaplaincy from parish ministry are only a few of the incongruities that I have witnessed at the intersection of Parish-based Ministry and Chaplaincy. Having served in both expressions of ministry and in the Academy, I can testify that there is acute vocational distinctiveness between the parish and Christian Academy and the chaplaincy. It seems to me there needs to be an understanding of how Christian ministry can serve in highly pluralistic communities — even those institutions that have taken anti-Christian stances — and maintain orthodoxy. In another book, I sought to present the essential chaplain ministry concept of "cooperation without compromise."[38] Undoubtedly cooperation without compromise is the single greatest operational value in chaplain ministry. For it allows the chaplain to conduct ministry among those who might even prefer that the institution prohibit his presence while being attentive to the *Imago Dei* in unbelievers, that is, the divinely created humanity of every individual, and the possibility of proclaiming the gospel of Jesus Christ. As important as cooperation without compromise is to the work of the chaplaincy it cannot be the bridge of mutual understanding that is needed to cross the breach between parish ministry and chaplain ministry. Our common faith calls us to consider the biblical-theological imperatives that grounds and guide chaplain ministry. That is the focus of the remainder of this monograph.

2

EXPOSITION ON A THEOLOGY OF THE CHAPLAINCY

FROM THE PASTORAL EPISTLES

It is no wonder that Presbyterian and Reformed Chaplaincy is so well represented in the Armed Forces, healthcare, corrections, first responders, and corporate sectors of society. The theological nature of Chaplaincy and its practice in the Reformed Churches have caused this unique ministry mission to flourish throughout church history. Chaplaincy as a distinct expression of ordained Christian pastoral ministry has its origins in the eighth century—its origins by the name of *Chaplaincy*, not its actual beginning (for that, we have evidence from earliest recorded instances of the Chaplaincy task in the Old Testament). The

following summary from a recent British
Army history clarifies:

> "Military chaplaincy was an ancient insti-
> tution even at the beginning of our pe-
> riod; in fact, the Latin term *cappellani* is
> thought to derive from the term *cappa*,
> namely the cape of St. Martin of Tours, a
> potent relic that was carried into battle by
> the Frankish kinds and which required
> the care of a dedicated band of clergy."[1]

Thus, Chaplains, as a term for clergy embedded in what we might call "closed end"
institutions; organizations like the military
and hospitals.[2] Though the term "chaplain"
existed since the eighth century A.D., English-speaking Christian ministry adapted the
term from Continental sources and expanded the role. Given Protestantism's even-
tual predominance in the English-speaking
peoples' history, the Chaplain became much
more than a lucky relic for war. Indeed, as
we will see, the Continental and British Isles
Reformed Chaplains were (and remain) notable for their three-fold influence among
those they served (those three biblical-theo-

logical truths are explored in this monograph). Moreover, Chaplains began to serve a variety of institutions, including corporate or commercial, if you prefer, healthcare, first responders, education (from primary to higher education), as well as military and naval sectors.

This monograph is not intended to chronicle the history of Chaplaincy in English-speaking peoples. Rather, we seek to establish a theology of Chaplaincy from the Holy Scriptures. Moreover, we will illustrate the theological truths with applied theology, the pastoral theology of Chaplaincy, as a recognized ministry of Word and Sacrament, with particular attention to the Presbyterian and Reformed churches.

Restating the Need for Understanding

We explored the reasons why a careful consideration of a theology of chaplaincy is need in Part I. However, given the possible misunderstandings between parish-based ministries and the chaplaincy, the case may be restated and, thus, reiterated.

Many chaplains express concern that

fellow ministers of Word and Sacrament don't understand their place in the larger Church. We present no research or citation beyond anecdotal evidence to support our suspicion. Anecdotal evidence is still evidence. So, for the sake of showing good faith, let us take these comments (made to me) at their word. The author has heard this many times in a career at the intersection of parish, academy, and chaplaincy. Interestingly, other ministers in other traditions and countries have voiced the same concern. Speaking broadly and out of concern, we might surmise the following:

- Parish ministry is understood to be the norm. Word and Sacrament ministry is exercised within the Christian community.
- Home and foreign missionaries are, likewise, extensions of a parish ministry with a focus, often, on establishing new Christian communities.

In Part II we will seek to deploy the writings of the Apostle Paul in the Pastoral Epistles (1 and 2 Timothy, Titus) to identify and discuss *four prominent features of a theology of chaplaincy*. We will also isolate *four vignettes from church history* that demonstrate the theological truth and the pastoral application of the respective features of that ministry called Chaplaincy.

The first unmistakable feature that establishes and supports Chaplaincy as a viable and necessary ministry in the Church is predictable, familiar, yet absolutely indispensable.

Chaplaincy is a supreme expression of Evangelism and Mission

The apostolic-like ministry of chaplaincy emphasizes evangelism and mission. The chaplain is an itinerant evangelist, ministering to unique areas of ministry on the move. In 2 Timothy 4:5, Paul urges Timothy to "do the work of an evangelist, fulfill your ministry." This call to evangelism and mission is exemplified by chaplains throughout church history, such as the missionary chaplains who served in military conflicts such as the Crusades and the Vietnam War. These chaplains ministered to soldiers, offering the hope of the Gospel in the midst of war and hardship. No less than the Westminster Assembly of Divines gave the powers of an evangelist to chaplains like the Welsh Puritan Vavasor Powell. While a pastor of the parish at Dartford, Kent, Powell spent many months away from his local ministry to serve as a Chaplain to Parliamentary forces. Higher history, like the actions of the Westminster Assembly, and lower history, the records of Dartford parish, support the Reformed understanding of Chaplaincy as an expression of the work of an evangelist. Yet, seventeenth-century English Calvinism was merely continuing a pastoral-theological application of mission in Reformed churches. Indeed, we can go back further than Seventeenth Century English Puritanism.

John Calvin and Chaplains

For one of the most notable examples of Reformed Chaplaincy—Protestant ministers of Word and Sacrament demonstrating incarnational presence and evangelistic outreach to a particular group defined by a corporate mission or work—we go to Geneva. Many have now written about the mission commitment of Calvin and other Reformers, with the former having supported work in Brazil. Calvin's dedication to sending ministers to live among others working in a closed group is supported by his theology of evangelism and missions. Concerning Daniel 12:3, the Swiss Reformer wrote, "God has deposited the teaching of his salvation with us, not for the purpose of ... keeping it to ourselves, but of our pointing out the way of salvation to all mankind. This, therefore, is the common duty of the children of God – to promote the salvation of their brethren." Thus, Calvin and other Reformers lived this theological vision by sending ministers to serve in closed-end groups. One of the most fascinating stories of John Calvin's commitment to the applied theology of chaplaincy occurred during the Geneva Plague.

"In 1542, there was an outbreak of the plague. The plague hospital was full. A Chaplain was required. The protestant minister Pierre Blanchet offered himself and was accepted by the Council. After a short time, the plague ceased, and Blanchett left the hospital. The plague broke out again in 1543. On May 1, Calvin announced to the council that Castellion, a minister, was ready to go as chaplain to the hospital. The Council accepted his offer, at the time censuring some ministers who were unwilling to go to the hospital. This was on May 2, but on the 11th, Castellion was superseded, and Blanchet reappointed. Blanchet, however, died, and on June 1, the Council ordered the ministers to meet and choose a chaplain, Mr. Calvin being excluded because he was required for the Church. The following week a chaplain was appointed, 'Mr. Calvin being excluded because he was required for the Church.'"

So, it is clear that Calvin both called and sent forth chaplains to institutions. Yet, there is more. For Calvin wrote about the necessity of chaplains and even considered that he should leave the local church to serve as a chaplain. John Calvin wrote a letter in October 1542 at the beginning of the plague,

> "If anything happens to Blanchett, I fear that after him, it will be my turn to run the risk . . . we cannot feel those who need our ministry more than others . . .

> As long as we are in this charge, I do not see how we could excuse or shells if, through fear of danger, we deprive of the help those who need it most."

Reformed ministers of Word and Sacrament, including Chaplain Pierre Blanchet, Chaplain Castellion, and, of course, the great Reformer John Calvin, are exemplars of a theology of the Chaplaincy at work.

Such groups included government exploration projects, merchant navies, and militias. In the case of sending ministers of Word and Sacrament to live among long-distance merchant ventures, a common practice for both Continental and British exploration, ministers of Word and Sacrament were not necessarily called "Chaplains." However, Chaplains, they were. They were ministers of the Gospel embedded in unique close-end communities, there to bring Word and Sacrament to the members of the exploration team as well as reaching new people groups. Are they Chaplains or missionaries? The answer is "Yes." The Reformed pastors were Chaplains, as we use the term, and they were missionaries. To the Reformers, they were just ministers of the Gospel. Indeed, our Chaplains today, whether in a hospital or on an aircraft carrier, or for that matter, like these Reformed Chaplains, embedded in a commercial venture, were Christian shepherds exercising ministry in extraordinary circumstances. Calvin did not speak of "corporate chaplaincy" or "healthcare" chaplaincy any more than he used the phrase "church planting." Yet he undeniably supported both.

The second salient feature in the theology of Chaplaincy is one of its most famous: "The Ministry of Presence." This designator recognizes an essential part of Chaplaincy and Gospel ministry:

Chaplaincy is a perceivable demonstration of the Incarnation

The Incarnation of our Lord and Savior Jesus Christ, God became Man without ceasing to be God, is an essential message of Christianity. "And the Word became flesh, and dwelt among us, and we saw His glory, glory as of the only begotten from the Father, full of grace and truth (John 1:14). In the unforgettable words of St. Paul, "He is the image of the invisible God, the firstborn of all creation" (Colossians 1:15). This message of the incarnation is at the core of our confession of faith:

> "What was from the beginning, what we have heard, what we have seen with our eyes, what we have looked at and touched with our hands, concerning the Word of Life— and the life was manifested, and we have seen and testify and proclaim to you the eternal life, which was with the Father and was manifested to us" (1 John 1:1-2).

The Church has understood Gospel ministry as a reflection of this vital teaching of the Gospel as well as the Christ-modeled method for conducting the Great Commission. We must become like those we minister to without ceasing to be the new creatures we are in Christ. This incarnational character of ministry is central to the work of the evangelist or missionary serving as a chaplain. Chaplaincy is a ministry embedded in a unique setting that is often insulated from the ordinary outreach of the local church. In 1 Timothy 1:3, Paul charges Timothy: "As I urged you when I was going to Macedonia, remain at Ephesus so that you may charge certain persons not to teach any different doctrine,"

Titus 2:7, Paul exhorts Titus to "show yourself in all respects to be a model of good works, and in your teaching show integrity, dignity." This emphasis on modeling the life of Christ among those whom we serve is reflected in the work of chaplains who minister in correctional institutions, hospitals, and other unique settings. In their "ministry of presence," our chaplains embody the presence of Christ in unique settings, offering comfort, guidance, and hope to those who are often unreached by others in the Church.

The Reformation enlivened all aspects of the pastoral task. It may be rightly stated that the Church had not known such active missionary zeal since the fall of Rome and, perhaps, the first century after Christ. The Reformed Church in the Netherlands is a remarkable example. Not only did the Reformation recovery of biblical truth and practice transform parish life but demonstrated a robust and even entrepreneurial spirit in missions and, in particular, the Chaplaincy. One example comes from the formation of the Dutch East India Company.

The imperial expansion of Great Britain saw the growth of the largest empire in human history. Undoubtedly, the charter of the East India Company, the world's first "corporation," was integral, if not the cause of, the British Empire's ascendancy.[3] The enterprise was a unique public-private partnership of not merely commerce and state but, in reality, company, crown, and Church. From its genesis on 31 December 1600, under Elizabeth I, the East India Company (EIC) articulated a mission to include the advancement of the gospel of Jesus Christ. It is a fact of history that Chaplains were employed by the enterprise from 1601-1858 (the remnants of the EIC lasted until 01 June 1874). The East India Company (called in successive periods the British East India Company, English East India Company, Governor and Company of Merchants of London Trading into the East Indies, and the United Company of Merchants of England Trading to the East Indies) was chartered for trade and for advancement of the Gospel. The EIC employed chaplains, Anglican, Presbyterian, and Congregationalist. Even the English Civil War (three wars were fought in what is recalled as 1639–1653 Wars of the Three Kingdoms) could not dampen the global trading company's aspirations. Despite the royalist leanings of the merchant class in England, Wales, Scotland, and Ireland, the company called Puritans to the chaplaincy. One Presbyterian, in particular, recorded his work as a Chaplain. His ministry with the East India Company—both as a corporate Chaplain and a naval Chaplain for the Merchant Navy — included the type of work that our PRCC Chaplains do today: serve the ministry needs of the employees and seek to evangelize those with whom British trade was established (principally, the various people groups in India).

The present ministry to corporate, healthcare, first responder, government, and Armed Forces sectors does not need a defense. Nevertheless, the annals of Presbyterian and Reformed church history offer irrefutable and plentiful evidence that both challenges the Church and justifies Chaplaincy.

Chaplaincy is an Undeniable Example of Intensive Shepherding

The phrase "ministry of presence" is one often heard when discussing chaplain ministry. The phrase intends to communicate more than physical presence. Rather a "ministry of presence" speaks to the intentionality and intensity of the chaplain's presence. The chaplain seeks to represent the Lord Jesus Christ as His ambassador, and to bring an incarnational message from God's Word to the people. Thus, chaplaincy is a highly focused ministry of pastoral care and counseling to a unique sector of society. Such intensity of ministry is urged in the Bible. For example, Peter, in 1 Peter 5:2-3, exhorts the elders:

"Shepherd the flock of God that is among you, exercising oversight, not under compulsion, but willingly, as God would have you; not for shameful gain, but eagerly; not domineering over those in your charge, but being examples to the flock."

The Pastoral Epistles are, likewise, replete with Paul's concern for intensive shepherding of the flock of Christ. In 2 Timothy 4:2-3 Paul admonishes Timothy: "Preach the word; be ready in season and out of season; reprove, rebuke, and exhort, with complete patience and teaching. For the time is coming when people will not endure sound teaching, but having itching ears they will accumulate for themselves teachers to suit their own passions."

Again, Paul wrote Titus that the nature of Christian shepherding requires a consecrated ministry:

"This is why I left you in Crete, so that you might put what remained into order, and appoint elders in every town as I directed you— if anyone is above reproach, the husband of one wife, and his children are believers and not open to the charge of debauchery or insubordination. For an overseer, as God's steward, must be above reproach. He must not be arrogant or quick-tempered or a drunkard or violent or greedy for gain, but hospitable, a lover of good, self-controlled, upright, holy, and disciplined" (Titus 1:5-9).

This passage shows Paul's concern for the appointment of elders in every town to shepherd the flock and ensure that they are led by those who are above reproach and capable of guiding them in righteousness. This emphasis on shepherding—qualified and tested ministers exercising faithful Gospel ministry on a personal level—is exemplified by chaplains who serve in the military, offering support to soldiers and their families in times of crisis and uncertainty. This is the ministry of presence: bringing the Word of God in the form of one set apart for Gospel ministry of Word and Sacrament.

One example of how Presbyterian and Reformed churches have supported "the ministry of presence" and how Chaplains have faithfully exercised this mission is the case of Dr. D. James Kennedy and Chaplain (Colonel) Dave Peterson (both men are now with the Lord). Dr. Kennedy knew Chaplain Peterson, who had preached at Coral Ridge Presbyterian Church. Dr. Kennedy, an enthusiastic advocate for Chaplaincy in all sectors, rallied his congregation to send bibles for Troops in the Persian Gulf. The campaign brought in an incredible number of Bibles. There were so many Bibles given by listeners to Truths that Transform radio ministry that they had to be shipped to Chaplain (Colonel) Peterson on multiple pallets. Since Coalition Forces were positioned on Arab Muslim land, the host government banned Bibles (as well as liquor and pornography). So, the pallets arrived in a less than conspicuous manner. There were twenty or more pallets of bibles, literally thousands of bibles, unloaded to the attention of Chaplain Peterson. At the next General's Staff Meeting, Normal Schwarzkopf (1934-2012), Commander of U. S. Central Command and the Commanding Officers of more than 700,000 American, British, and other Coalition national forces, held the Chaplain's section report for last. As General Schwarzkopf turned to Chaplain Peterson, he cut off any report with a report of his own. As Dave Peterson related the story to Dr. Kennedy and me in a private conversation at Coral Ridge Presbyterian Church the legendary four-star general looked at his Chaplain, for whom he held great respect and affection, and snorted but clearly (words to this effect), "Chaplain, I have one word for you. We appreciate the American people's kindness and concern for our Soldiers' spiritual welfare. However, as you know, we are under a special agreement with the Saudis. So, Chaplain, I want you to get rid of those Bibles. Is that clear?" Chaplain Peterson stood at attention with the senior British Chaplain and other national Chaplains behind them. "Sir," he began and was cut off. "Chaplain?" The general's intonation came with an authoritative pause. "Chaplain do not tell me how you do it. Just do it." Chaplain Peterson responded, "Yes, Sir!" The General Staff meeting was dismissed by Schwarzkopf. Chaplain Peterson told his colleagues, "Men, we need to have a prayer meeting ASAP. That's an order." Thus, the American Chaplain gathered with Chaplains from European and British Commonwealth nations. And they did pray. Chaplain Peterson reflected on that prayer meeting, "We admitted to the Lord that we did not know what to do. We wanted to honor both the promise made by our governments to the host country and honor God and His Word.

We left the meeting without a clear understanding of what was next. We knew the principles in play. We just didn't know the next move." Dave Peterson laughed in wonder as he related what happened next. "Well, the Lord heard our prayers. As you might remember, Iraqi soldiers began turning themselves in without a fight. Hundreds and hundreds of them crossed the lines and became Prisoners of War right there in the desert. Almost to a man, the Iraqis wanted food and drink, and they wanted, you guessed it, a Bible! Not only was there a revival of Iraqis in our POW facilities, with baptisms happening daily, but Coalition Forces wanted the Bibles. At the next General Staff Meeting, General Schwarzkopf asked me, "Dave, did you get rid of those Bibles?" Before Chaplain Peterson could reply, the General put his hand up, palm facing Chaplain Peterson, in a "Stop where you are!" gesture. "Ugh, ugh. I said don't tell me." Chaplain Peterson popped to attention. "Yes, Sir!" And the smile between the two men communicated more than words.

As I read stories of the astounding numbers of Muslims coming to Christ, literally "turning themselves in" to local clergy, saying that the Lord guided them to confess their faith and to be baptized, I cannot help but wonder, "Lord, is this the fruit of all of those Bibles from those weeks in the desert in the early months of 1991?"

The story is not only real but instructive. Chaplains, whether ministering to Soldiers in war or ministering to emergency medical teams in an urban war zone, preaching Christ (as I have done) to death row inmates in a correctional institution, or any of the other Chaplain ministry sectors, Chaplains can "be there" when needed. They are granted unimaginable opportunities to shepherd lost souls to the Good Shepherd and to guide God's Flock through nourishment in Word, Sacrament, and Prayer.

Chaplaincy is Uniquely Prophetic:

By *prophetic,* we mean "proclaiming the Word of God in its ethical and moral dimensions to respective groups of people in need of guidance." In our definition, a Chaplain giving biblical-ethical counsel to a military officer making a battle plan is *prophetic*. A

Healthcare Chaplain providing Christian moral guidance to a surgeon seeking counsel is also *prophetic*. A Chaplain in a correctional institution supporting a task force to write a policy for detainees is an expression of *prophetic* ministry.

Paul called Timothy to be strong in his ministry to Ephesus. There were errors of theology as well as practice. Timothy needed to "remain at Ephesus" to address these matters with sound teaching.

> "As I urged you when I was going to Macedonia, remain at Ephesus so that you may charge certain persons not to teach any different doctrine, nor to devote themselves to myths and endless genealogies, which promote speculations rather than the stewardship from God that is by faith" (1 Timothy 1:3-4).

> "If you put these things before the brothers, you will be a good servant of Christ Jesus, being trained in the words of the faith and of the good doctrine that you have followed. Have nothing to do with irreverent, silly myths. Rather

train yourself for godliness" (1 Timothy 4:6-7).

"And the Lord's servant must not be quarrelsome but kind to everyone, able to teach, patiently enduring evil, correcting his opponents with gentleness. God may perhaps grant them repentance leading to a knowledge of the truth, and they may come to their senses and escape from the snare of the devil, after being captured by him to do his will" (2 Timothy 2:24-26).

Thus, Chaplaincy is a bearer of the moral truths of God interpreted, applied, and shared. The Chaplain is a uniquely placed authority and asset to provide Christian, biblical, and Reformed ethics to leaders facing diverse ethical dilemmas. In 1 Timothy 4:16, Paul exhorts Timothy to "keep a close watch on yourself and on the teaching. Persist in this, for by so doing, you will save both yourself and your hearers." This call to uphold Christian teaching and ethics is reflected in the work of chaplains who serve in corporate and first responder settings, offering guidance and wisdom to leaders facing ethical challenges.

I offer an illustration of the Chaplain as *prophet*—i.e., public theologian—from my own experience—not in *my* stand for truth in the trenches but as one who instructed those who were. Indeed, I served (with other PRCC Chaplains) on faculty at the U. S. Chaplain Center and School in Fort Jackson, South Carolina. A significant component of my Chaplain work was designing, writing, and delivering courses on biblical ethics, education, homiletics, and liturgics. In the ethics courses I examined moral frameworks that invariably exist in the hearts and minds of those we serve. I sought to compare and contrast these systems with the transcendent and theistic ethics based on Scripture and, in particular, the ethics of the Word of God. My teaching led me to instruct U.S. and British Chaplains in a special joint ethical training in Washington DC. My work was subsequently expanded and published as a book.[4] The fact that a PRCC Chaplain could navigate the sometimes-treacherous ledge of secularism and naturalism that pervades present-day government structures may be an example. However, the greater takeaway concerning prophetic Gospel ministry is this: I regularly counseled (a large number, perhaps even hundreds) Chaplains who were in the field, in the battle, who served their commanders by providing biblical-ethical counsel. The case study is, thus, extensive. It includes significant pastoral moments when PRCC Chaplains spoke biblical truth to a higher-ranking commanding. Often Chaplains do this at risk of losing their positions. Such examples are fraught with danger on numerous fronts but are one of the main reasons the Chaplain is present in Armed Forces operations (the same vocational dynamic exists in other Chaplaincy sectors like healthcare, first responders, correctional, corporate, and education). In one case, a Chaplain in Iraq sensed a growing spirit of retribution among Soldiers following a roadside bombing that cost the lives of brothers in the unit. The Chaplain also sensed that the commander, an otherwise strong and respected leader, was unwittingly but nevertheless really allowing a base feeling of retaliation to fester. While some might be tempted to appreciate such collective passions as a helpful instrument engendering *esprit de corps*, the truth is that such emotions can become ungovernable passions leading to vigilantism and even war crimes. The Chaplain recognized the approaching danger and respectfully aired his concern to the commander. The Chaplain cited the moral danger that could risk the integrity of a "just war" operation and provided biblical-theological Christian ethics that supported U. S. Army battlefield doctrine. The Chaplain also recognized the personal spiritual battle that was undoubtedly present in the commander (who had to write a letter to the widows of the Soldiers lost). The PRCC Chaplain's counsel was not confrontational (not "speaking truth to power") but rather pastoral. He concluded with prayer and offered to support the commander in any way the commander thought best. In this case, the commander of the unit was aware of the feelings and admitted that he shared them. However, he responded to the concern of the Chaplain and addressed the matter with wisdom and clarity. The commander met with his staff, disseminated an authoritative call for Soldier professionalism, and asked the Chaplain to be available to support the communication with a time of counseling as well as a special chapel service. The result? No news was made. No crimes were committed. Instead, the unit conducted its mission with dignity and effectiveness. There was no Abu Ghraib atrocity thanks to one PRCC Chaplain who became a public theologian— speaking a prophetic word from God's Word. We have a name for that kind of heroism: *pastor.*

3

CONCLUSIONS

The theological nature of chaplaincy as a mission of the church emphasizes evangelism and mission, incarnation, pastoral care and counseling, and the bearing of moral truths. Examples from Presbyterian and Reformed church history illustrate how chaplains have embodied these essential "Word and Sacrament" commitments in unique and challenging ministry settings, from ministers bearing witness to Christ and serving the unique spiritual needs of offering the hope of the Gospel to those often overlooked or marginalized. The call to chaplaincy is unique and remarkably missional, inviting ministers to minister

Word, Sacrament, and Prayer to those in need, identifying with the group in their mission, and serving as evangelists of the Church of our Lord Jesus Christ.

The future of chaplain ministry is as secure as the need to find meaning for life and beyond death in populations within closed-end institutions "outside of the gate."[1] The question of chaplain ministry is not one of validity. It is. The incongruities between parish-based ministry and chaplaincy are real but are, also, bridged by the exposition of the Word of God. The question that remains is how dedicated we are to becoming a field-preaching ministry in the passing years of the Twenty-first century. If we choose to follow the Lord Jesus as His ambassadors in chaplain ministry, like Calvin and a host of other Reformed ministers and ministries, then we will find that the widening secularization of the West will have a concurrent cry for ministers to come and help make sense of life without God. The situation is put well by a British missiologist:

So, in addition to being a ministry that begins with traditional pastoral care, beyond the borders of the Church and to the widest possible community, chaplaincy also meets a very modern challenge of a society that in multiple ways is abandoning religion.

The practical theological challenge to our churches and to the whole Church is not whether we involve ourselves in a mission within secular contexts, institutions and the whole of society; the challenge is how will we choose to do this with enough resources and commitment to make chaplaincy effective and secure ...[2]

The theology of chaplaincy is rooted in the soil whereupon our Savior walked. Our ministry is nurtured by the Incarnation of our God and Savior Jesus Christ, His presence among us, His sacrificial death on the cross for us, His resurrection, ascension, and mandate given to us to "Go into all the world ..."

Chaplaincy is now flowering in a most unusual season. But then again chaplaincy has always flourished in the paradoxical places of life. We go there because like John Donne we are "involved in mankind," and we are committed to the theological truths that "... All occasions invite his mercies, and all times are his seasons."[3]

NOTES

1. Why a Theology of Chaplaincy is Needed

1. Victoria Slater, *Chaplaincy Ministry and the Mission of the Church* (London: SCM Press, 2015), 125, https://books.google.com/books?id=MsNqCg AAQBAJ.
2. Revd Dr Christopher Swift, Revd Canon Dr Andrew Todd, and Revd Dr Mark Cobb, *A Handbook of Chaplaincy Studies: Understanding Spiritual Care in Public Places* (Ashgate Publishing, Ltd., 2015), 13.
3. See, e.g., the Barna report: Barna Group Staff Writers, "Pastors Share Top Reasons They've Considered Quitting Ministry in the Past Year," Barna Group, accessed May 10, 2023, https://www.barna. com/research/pastors-quitting-ministry/.
4. Chris Meinzer, "MDiv Enrollment Declines While MA and DMin Enrollments Grow among ATS Schools," *Colloquy Online*, no. February (2023): 1–2, p. 1, https://www.ats.edu/files/galleries/mdiv-enroll ment-declines.pdf.
5. Meinzer, "MDiv Enrollment Declines," 2023.
6. Wendy Cadge et al., "Training Chaplains and Spiritual Caregivers: The Emergence and Growth of Chaplaincy Programs in Theological Education," *Pastoral Psychology* 69, no. 3 (June 1, 2020): 187–208, citing p. 187, https://doi.org/10.1007/s11089-020-00906-5.
7. Cadge et al, "Training Chaplains," *Pastoral Psychology*, 207.

8. See Dr Justo L. Gonzalez, *The History of Theological Education* (Nashville: Abingdon Press, 2015). See, also, my research which validates a case for Dr. Gonzalez's concerns and is supportive of a pastoral model combining scholarship and a carefully structured supervised ministry with theological reflection: Michael Milton, "Reimagining Pastoral Education and Training: Defeating Pastoral Burnout and Dropout Through Uniting the University Model, the Apprenticeship Model, and Multi-Model Theological Higher Education," Theology and Religious Studies (ResearchGate, May 14, 2022), https://doi.org/10.6084/m9.figshare.19858144.v1.

9. Cadge et al, "Training Chaplains," *Pastoral Psychology*, 187.

10. See "Marsh Center," B. H. Carroll Theological Seminary, accessed May 13, 2023, https://bhcarroll.edu/about/organizations-partners/marsh-center/.

11. The author founded a Chaplain Center at RTS-Charlotte, with an emphasis in chaplaincy within the M.Div. degree. I did so while Chancellor-President of Reformed Theological Seminary. Since my retirement, the seminary leadership shifted emphasis. Chaplain ministries at Southwestern Baptist Theological Seminary, Carol Theological Seminary, Liberty Seminary, and Gordon-Conwell Theological Seminary are notable for their attentiveness to chaplain ministry in the Master of Divinity and in specialized Master of Arts programs. Furthermore, each of these, along with Erskine, offers doctoral level programs with a chaplain emphasis.

12. See Peter Somers Heslam and Abraham Kuyper, *Creating a Christian Worldview: Abraham Kuyper's*

Lectures on Calvinism (Grand Rapids: W.B. Eerdmans, 1998), 88.

13. See Jessica R. Joustra and Robert J. Joustra, *Calvinism for a Secular Age: A Twenty-First Century Reading of Abraham Kuyper's Stone Lectures* (InterVarsity Press, 2022).

14. H. Richard Niebuhr. *Christ and Culture.* New York: Harper & Row, 1951

15. See, e.g., Stavros Kofinas, "Chaplaincy in Europe," *Southern Medical Journal*, June 2006, Gale Academic OneFile, https://link.gale.com/apps/doc/A148139445/AONE?u=anon~5cac341d&sid=google Scholar&xid=86417b58.

16. See Lene Kühle and Henrik Reintoft Christensen, "One to Serve Them All: The Growth of Chaplaincy in Public Institutions in Denmark," *Social Compass* 66, no. 2 (June 2019): 182–97, https://doi.org/10.1177/0037768619833310.

17. This present-day trend must be addressed, firstly, in research. We need to understand what factors are triggering such angst and causing an exodus from the local pastorate. I have sought to contribute to the dialogue about this crisis with evidence-based research concerning one of those factors: preparation for pastoral ministry. See Michael A. Milton, "Reimagining Pastoral Education and Training" (Doctoral dissertation, Due West, SC, Erskine Theological Seminary, 2022), https://www.proquest.com/openview/4ba20c8d d840bababecdc07be20d198d/1?pq-origsite= gscholar&cbl=18750&diss=y. See, also, the research: Michael Milton, "Reimagining Pastoral Education and Training: Defeating Pastoral Burnout and Dropout Through Uniting the University Model, the Apprenticeship Model, and Multi-Model Theological Higher Education," Theology and Reli-

gious Studies (ResearchGate.net, May 14, 2022), https://doi.org/10.6084/m9.figshare.19858144.v1.

18. Personal interview with Rev. Dr. James Carter, Executive Director and Endorser for the PRCC, January 2023.

19. On "post-secularism" see, e.g., Jürgen Habermas, "Notes on Post-secular Society," *New Perspectives Quarterly* 25, no. 4 (2008): 17–29. See, also, the collection of contemporary scholarly thought on post secularism in

20. In this paper we use the term, "parish," or the phrase, "parish-based ministry" to refer to a constituted local church and its community mission. Thus, the term is used not as a jurisdiction but an area of ministry. See its use in my book: *Deep Roots: A Biblical and Theological Framework for Church Planting.* Weddington, NC: Bethesda Publishing Group, 2018. For a Reformed understanding of "parish" as describing a comprehensive evangelistic undertaking see my posting, "What is Parish Ministry?" Tryon, NC: Faithforliving.org, February 22, 2016, https://michaelmilton.org/2016/02/22/what-is-parish-ministry/.

21. Habermas delivered these remarks when he received the German Peace Prize in 2003. Portions of his speech are recorded in Jürgen Habermas and Ciaran P. Cronin, *An Awareness of What Is Missing: Faith and Reason in a Post-Secular Age* (Wiley, 2010), 6.

22. The phrase "theater of the absurd," coined by literary writer Martin Esslin, refers to the arts and drama *nouveau* that appeared after WWI. In particular, a Parisian group that included the Irish author Samuel Beckett ("Waiting for Godot"). The phrase came to embody the postmodern approach to utter meaninglessness in life. See the book by

Esslin Martin Esslin, *The Theatre of the Absurd* (New York: Knopf Doubleday Publishing Group, 2009). See, also, my commentary on literary reactions to the failure of modernity (rationalism) in Michael A. Milton, *From Flanders Fields to the Moviegoer: Philosophical Foundations for a Transcendent Ethical Framework* (Eugene, OR: Wipf and Stock Publishers, 2019).

23. Habermas, *An Awareness,* 9.
24. James Davison Hunter, *To Change the World: The Irony, Tragedy and Possibility of Christianity in the Late Modern World* (New York: Oxford University Press USA, 2010).
25. Miroslav Volf, *A Public Faith: How Followers of Christ Should Serve the Common Good* (Brazos Press, 2011), 96.
26. See Émile Durkheim. *The Elementary Forms of Religious Life.* United Kingdom: Oxford University Press, 2001.
27. James P. Walsh, "Holy Time and Sacred Space in Puritan New England," *American Quarterly* 32, no. 1 (1980): 79–95, p. 79, https://doi.org/10.2307/2712497. For further studies on the philosophy of appropriating meaning to time or space see
28. Jean Holm and John Bowker, *Sacred Place*, Douglas Davies, "Christianity" (Bloomsbury Publishing, 2001), 35.
29. Davies, "Christianity" in Sacred Place, 47.
30. Notes on Spurgeon from Terry D. Hale, "The Spurgeon Library | From Mentone to Norwood: The Final Journey of C. H. Spurgeon," Database, The Spurgeon Center, January 31, 2022, https://www.spurgeon.org/resource-library/blog-entries/from-mentone-to-norwood-the-final-journey-of-c-h-spurgeon/. The illustration given in this is most personal. When I was ordained as a minister in the

Presbyterian Church in America (PCA), I journeyed to Norwood Cemetery. I sat before the mausoleum of the "Prince of Preachers" to ask God for a thread from the mantle of Spurgeon (for I knew that without God's help, I could not wear more than that, not an exercise in faux humility, but an accurate assessment of my temperament and spiritual sanctification).

31.

32. My assertion is not intended to dismiss the concept of "sacred space," or the idea of "consecration," or "dedication." I hold that we have often erred too far on dismissing the sanctifying value of such concepts (concepts learned from God and His Word). So, we recognize a valuable "theology of place." Thus, I am arguing that the Bible does not teach there is moral virtue to be gained by such distinctives. For a scholarly treatment of the sociology of knowledge see Peter L. Berger and Thomas Luckmann, *The Social Construction of Reality: A Treatise in the Sociology of Knowledge* (Knopf Doubleday Publishing Group, 1967). For a comparison and contrast of sociology see Scott Monsma, "On the Journey: Reflecting on the Intersections of Sociology and Christianity," *Journal of Sociology and Christianity* 10, no. 1 (2020): 23–25.

33. Forensic investigation of even the purest Presbyterian polities undoubtedly discovers a "superintendent" or sole evangelist in its organizational chromosome lineage. It is from these individuals invested with the jurisdictional authority to preach, administer the sacraments, and establish self-governing, connectional Christian communities that "denominations" grow. No greater example is the history of the Church of Scotland and its subsidiary movements. See Ian Hazlett, *A Com-*

panion to the Reformation in Scotland, c.1525–1638: Frameworks of Change and Development (Leiden, Netherlands: Brill, 2021).

34. David W. Miller, Faith Wambura Ngunjiri, and James D. Lorusso, "'The Suits Care about Us': Employee Perceptions of Workplace Chaplains," *Journal of Management, Spirituality & Religion* 15, no. 5 (October 20, 2018): 377–97, https://doi.org/10.1080/14766086.2018.1501414.

35. For insight on Paul's tentmaking as a missional strategy see Joel Lohr, "He Identified with the Lowly and Became a Slave to All: Paul's Tentmaking as a Strategy for Mission," *Currents in Theology and Mission* 34, no. 3 (June 1, 2007): 179–87, https://scholarlycommons.pacific.edu/ed-facarti cles/24. For the sociological phenomena of Paul moving from one "class" (learned, urbane) to another (laborer) see Todd D. Still, "Did Paul Loathe Manual Labor? Revisiting the Work of Ronald F. Hock on the Apostle's Tentmaking and Social Class," *Journal of Biblical Literature* 125, no. 4 (2006): 781–95, https://doi.org/10.2307/27638405.

36. Amos tended sycamore fruit. The process for preparing the red Sycamore figs involves scraping the figs to force ripening. For an agricultural reflection on the process see Athanasios Theologis, "One Rotten Apple Spoils the Whole Bushel: The Role of Ethylene in Fruit Ripening," *Cell* 70, no. 2 (July 1992): 181–84, https://doi.org/10.1016/0092-8674(92)90093-R. For a review of issues in the study of Amos see Gerhard F. Hasel, *Understanding the Book of Amos: Basic Issues in Current Interpretations* (Wipf and Stock Publishers, 2019).

37. See James Francis and Leslie J. Francis, *Tentmaking: Perspectives on Self-Supporting Ministry* (Gracewing Publishing, 1998).

38. Michael A. Milton, *Cooperation Without Compromise (Stapled Booklet): Faithful Gospel Witness in a Pluralistic Setting* (Eugene, OR: Wipf and Stock Publishers, 2007).

2. Exposition On A Theology Of The Chaplaincy

1. Michael Francis Snape, *The Royal Army Chaplains' Department, 1796-1953: Clergy Under Fire* (Woodbridge, Suffolk: Boydell Press, 2008), 15.
2. "Closed end" institutions are those enterprises characterized by a singular métier, often segregated from other sectors of society by its distinctive mission, mobility, isolation, or professional association. The military and naval forces are closed end, i.e., not open to all, organized by a highly trained professional officer and non-commissioned officer class, and while in service of their mission, somewhat inescapable. Hospitals are, likewise, closed in from both a professional capacity as well as its unique mission in society. The degree of these singularities has always varied by sector. For example, the British East India Company, requiring what we, today, call "corporate chaplains," was quite closed ended in terms of isolation, mobility, and professional association (e.g., the British Merchant Navy) but not so much in its essential commercial mission.
3. See, e.g., Tirthankar Roy, *The East India Company: The World's Most Powerful Corporation* (Allen Lane, 2012), x.
4. M. A. Milton, *From Flanders Fields to the Moviegoer: Philosophical Foundations for a Transcendent Ethical Framework* (Eugene, OR: Wipf & Stock, 2019),

https://books.google.com/books?id=Pka6Dw
AAQBAJ.

3. Conclusions

1. See my conclusions in Michael A. Milton, "The Future of Chaplain Ministry in the United States Armed Forces," *The Chaplain Corps Journal*, Summer 2015, 34-37, https://cdm16040.contentdm. oclc.org/digital/collection/p16040coll4/id/11.
2. Robert Jones, "Characteristics of Chaplaincy," *Epworth Review*, December 2010, 5–9, p. 8, https:// www.methodist.org.uk/media/2572/epworth-re view-characteristicsofchaplaincy-1210.pdf.
3. John Donne's reference to being "involved in mankind" is taken from his Sermon Seventeen in *Death's Duel,* 1623. See, e.g., John Donne, *John Donne: Selections from Divine Poems, Sermons, Devotions, and Prayers* (Paulist Press, 1990), 58. Donne's line, "All times are His seasons," is taken from John Donne's Christmas Day sermon, 1624. See John Donne, *John Donne's Sermons on the Psalms and Gospels: With a Selection of Prayers and Meditations* (University of California Press, 2003), 182.

BIBLIOGRAPHY

ATS Editors. "Pathways for Tomorrow - Advisory Committee." Accessed May 10, 2023. https://www.ats.edu/Pathways-for-Tomorrow-Advisory-Committee.

Barna Group Staff Writers. "Pastors Share Top Reasons They've Considered Quitting Ministry in the Past Year." Barna Group. Accessed May 10, 2023. https://www.barna.com/research/pastors-quitting-ministry/.

Berger, Peter L., and Thomas Luckmann. *The Social Construction of Reality: A Treatise in the Sociology of Knowledge*. Knopf Doubleday Publishing Group, 1967.

Cadge, Wendy, Irene Elizabeth Stroud, Patricia K. Palmer, George Fitchett, Trace Haythorn, and Casey Clevenger. "Training Chaplains and Spiritual Caregivers: The Emergence and Growth of Chaplaincy Programs in Theological Education." *Pastoral Psychology* 69, no. 3 (June 1, 2020): 187–208. https://doi.org/10.1007/s11089-020-00906-5.

Caperon, J., A. Todd, J. Walters, M. Seeley, B. Ryan, M. Whipp, C. Bradley, and R. Williams. *A Christian Theology of Chaplaincy*. Jessica Kingsley Publishers, 2017. https://books.google.com/books?id=MBaXDgAAQBAJ.

Caperon, John, Andrew Todd, and James Walters. *A Christian Theology of Chaplaincy*. Jessica Kingsley Publishers, 2017.

Dickens Jr, William E. *Answering the Call: The Story of the US Military Chaplaincy from the Revolution through the Civil War*. Universal-Publishers, 1999.

Donne, John. *John Donne: Selections from Divine Poems, Sermons, Devotions, and Prayers*. Paulist Press, 1990.

———. *John Donne's Sermons on the Psalms and Gospels: With a Selection of Prayers and Meditations*. University of California Press, 2003.

Dreher, Rod. "Chaplain Peterson, Prophet." *National Review* (blog), May 11, 2004. https://www.nationalreview.com/corner/chaplain-peterson-prophet-rod-dreher/.

Durkheim, Émile, Carol Cosman, and Mark Sidney Cladis. *The Elementary Forms of Religious Life*. Oxford University Press, 2001. https://books.google.com/books?id=3j5tyWkEZSYC.

Eade, John. "Parish and Pilgrimage in a Changing Europe." *Migration, Transnationalism and Catholicism: Global Perspectives*, 2016, 75–92.

Editors at the Marsh Center. "Marsh Center." B. H. Carroll Theological Seminary. Accessed May 13, 2023. https://bhcarroll.edu/about/organizations-partners/marsh-center/.

Esslin, Martin. *The Theatre of the Absurd*. New York: Knopf Doubleday Publishing Group, 2009.

Fitchett, George. "Recent Progress in Chaplaincy-Related Research." *Journal of Pastoral Care & Counseling* 71, no. 3 (2017): 163–75.

Ford, Tim, and Alexander Tartaglia. "The Development, Status, and Future of Healthcare Chaplaincy." *Southern Medical Journal* 99, no. 6 (2006): 675–80.

Francis, James, and Leslie J. Francis. *Tentmaking: Per-*

spectives on Self-Supporting Ministry*. Gracewing Publishing, 1998.

Furseth, Inger. "Secularization and the Role of Religion in State Institutions." *Social Compass* 50, no. 2 (2003): 191–202.

Gonzalez, Dr Justo L. *The History of Theological Education*. Nashville: Abingdon Press, 2015.

Habermas, Jürgen. "Notes on Post-secular Society." *New Perspectives Quarterly* 25, no. 4 (2008): 17–29.

Habermas, Jürgen, and Ciaran P. Cronin. *An Awareness of What Is Missing: Faith and Reason in a Post-Secular Age*. Wiley, 2010. https://books.google.com/books?id=ZBXIDTLiG2MC.

Hale, Terry D. "The Spurgeon Library | From Mentone to Norwood: The Final Journey of C. H. Spurgeon." Database. The Spurgeon Center, January 31, 2022. https://www.spurgeon.org/resource-library/blog-entries/from-mentone-to-norwood-the-final-journey-of-c-h-spurgeon/.

Hasel, Gerhard F. *Understanding the Book of Amos: Basic Issues in Current Interpretations*. Wipf and Stock Publishers, 2019.

Hazlett, Ian. *A Companion to the Reformation in Scotland, c.1525–1638: Frameworks of Change and Development*. Leiden, Netherlands: Brill, 2021.

Hersh, Seymour M. "Chain of Command." *The New Yorker*, May 9, 2004. https://www.newyorker.com/magazine/2004/05/17/chain-of-command-2.

Heslam, Peter Somers, and Abraham Kuyper. *Creating a Christian Worldview: Abraham Kuyper's Lectures on Calvinism*. Grand Rapids: W.B. Eerdmans, 1998. https://books.google.com/books?id=iV3ZAAAAMAAJ.

Holm, Jean, and John Bowker. *Sacred Place*. Bloomsbury Publishing, 2001.

Holm, Neil. "Practicing the Ministry of Presence in Chaplaincy." *Journal of Christian Education*, no. 3 (2009): 29–42.

Hunter, James Davison. *To Change the World: The Irony, Tragedy and Possibility of Christianity in the Late Modern World*. OUP USA, 2010.

Irwin, C. H. *John Calvin: The Man and His Work*. Religious Tract Society, 1909. https://books.google.com/books?id=TZ9EAQAAMAAJ.

Jones, Ian. "Cardiff Centre for Chaplaincy Studies – WMCFEC." Cardiff: The Church of England, May 20, 2014. https://wmcfec.org.uk/tag/cardiff-centre-for-chaplaincy-studies/.

Jones, Robert. "Characteristics of Chaplaincy." *Epworth Review*, December 2010, 5–9. https://www.methodist.org.uk/media/2572/epworth-review-characteristic sofchaplaincy-1210.pdf.

Joustra, Jessica R., and Robert J. Joustra. *Calvinism for a Secular Age: A Twenty-First Century Reading of Abraham Kuyper's Stone Lectures*. InterVarsity Press, 2022.

Kofinas, Stavros. "Chaplaincy in Europe." *Southern Medical Journal*, June 2006. Gale Academic OneFile. https://link.gale.com/apps/doc/A148139445/AONE?u=anon~5cac341d&sid=googleScholar&xid=86417b58.

Kühle, Lene, and Henrik Reintoft Christensen. "One to Serve Them All: The Growth of Chaplaincy in Public Institutions in Denmark." *Social Compass* 66, no. 2 (June 2019): 182–97. https://doi.org/10.1177/0037768619833310.

Kuyper, Abraham. "Lectures on Calvinism," n.d.

Kverndal, Roald. *Seamen's Missions: Their Origin and Early Growth*. William Carey Library, 1986.

Lawson, P. *The East India Company: A History*. Taylor & Francis, 2014. https://books.google.com/books?id=PQOtAgAAQBAJ.

Lohr, Joel. "He Identified with the Lowly and Became a Slave to All: Paul's Tentmaking as a Strategy for Mission." *Currents in Theology and Mission* 34, no. 3 (June 1, 2007): 179–87. https://scholarlycommons.pacific.edu/ed-facarticles/24.

Meinzer, Chris. "MDiv Enrollment Declines While MA and DMin Enrollments Grow among ATS Schools." *Colloquy Online*, no. February (2023): 1–2. https://www.ats.edu/files/galleries/mdiv-enrollment-declines.pdf.

Miller, David W., Faith Wambura Ngunjiri, and James D. Lorusso. "'The Suits Care about Us': Employee Perceptions of Workplace Chaplains." *Journal of Management, Spirituality & Religion* 15, no. 5 (October 20, 2018): 377–97. https://doi.org/10.1080/14766086.2018.1501414.

Milton, M. A. *From Flanders Fields to the Moviegoer: Philosophical Foundations for a Transcendent Ethical Framework*. Eugene, OR: Wipf & Stock, 2019. https://books.google.com/books?id=Pka6DwAAQBAJ.

Milton, Michael. "Reimagining Pastoral Education and Training: Defeating Pastoral Burnout and Dropout Through Uniting the University Model, the Apprenticeship Model, and Multi-Model Theological Higher Education." Theology and Religious Studies. Researchgate, May 14, 2022. https://doi.org/10.6084/m9.figshare.19858144.v1.

Milton, Michael A. *Cooperation Without Compromise (Stapled Booklet): Faithful Gospel Witness in a Pluralistic Setting*. Eugene, OR: Wipf and Stock Publishers, 2007.

———. *From Flanders Fields to the Moviegoer: Philosophical Foundations for a Transcendent Ethical Framework*. Eugene, OR: Wipf and Stock Publishers, 2019.

———. "Reimagining Pastoral Education and Training." Doctoral dissertation, Erskine Theological Seminary, 2022. https://www.proquest.com/openview/4ba20c8dd840babababecdc07be20d198d/1?pq-origsite=gscholar&cbl=18750&diss=y.

———. "The Future of Chaplain Ministry in the United States Armed Forces." *The Chaplain Corps Journal*, Summer 2015, 34–37. https://cdm16040.contentdm.oclc.org/digital/collection/p16040coll4/id/11.

Monsma, Scott. "On the Journey: Reflecting on the Intersections of Sociology and Christianity." *Journal of Sociology and Christianity* 10, no. 1 (2020): 23–25.

O'Connor, D. *Chaplains of the East India Company, 1601-1858*. Bloomsbury Academic, 2012. https://books.google.com/books?id=nZXBeFowpV8C.

Peng-Keller, Simon, and David Neuhold. "Charting Spiritual Care: The Emerging Role of Chaplaincy Records in Global Health Care," 2020.

Poncin, Emmanuelle, Pierre-Yves Brandt, François Rouiller, Mario Drouin, and Zhargalma Dandarova Robert. "Mapping the Healthcare Chaplaincy Literature: An Analytical Review of Publications Authored by Chaplains and Theologians between 2000 and 2018." *Journal of Health Care Chaplaincy* 26, no. 1 (2020): 16–44.

Roy, T. *The East India Company: The World's Most Pow-

erful Corporation. Allen Lane, 2012. https://books. google.com/books?id=yTnm_D8wsrwC.

Samuel, Shanti. "Developing a Community Chaplaincy Ministry: Through a Need Satisfaction Care Model for a Native Language Church." *Doctoral Dissertations and Projects*, March 2, 2023. https://digitalcom mons.liberty.edu/doctoral/4162.

Sargent, J. *The Life of the Rev. T. T. Thomason, Chaplain to the East-India Company*. Appleton, 1833. https:// books.google.com/books?id=6sRoAAAAcAAJ.

Slater, Victoria. *Chaplaincy Ministry and the Mission of the Church*. London: SCM Press, 2015. https://books. google.com/books?id=MsNqCgAAQBAJ.

Snape, Michael Francis. *The Royal Army Chaplains' Department, 1796-1953: Clergy Under Fire*. Woodbridge, Suffolk: Boydell Press, 2008. https://books.google. com/books?id=oEWYDTHXSbYC.

Stahl, Ronit Y. *Enlisting Faith: How the Military Chaplaincy Shaped Religion and State in Modern America*. Harvard University Press, 2017.

Stifoss-Hanssen, Hans, Lars Johan Danbolt, and Hilde Frøkedal. "Chaplaincy in Northern Europe: An Overview from Norway." *Tidsskrift for Praktisk Teologi* 36, no. 2 (2019): 60–70.

Still, Todd D. "Did Paul Loathe Manual Labor? Revisiting the Work of Ronald F. Hock on the Apostle's Tentmaking and Social Class." *Journal of Biblical Literature* 125, no. 4 (2006): 781–95. https://doi.org/10. 2307/27638405.

Swift, Revd Dr Christopher, Revd Canon Dr Andrew Todd, and Revd Dr Mark Cobb. *A Handbook of Chaplaincy Studies: Understanding Spiritual Care in Public Places*. Ashgate Publishing, Ltd., 2015.

Theologis, Athanasios. "One Rotten Apple Spoils the Whole Bushel: The Role of Ethylene in Fruit Ripening." *Cell* 70, no. 2 (July 1992): 181–84. https://doi.org/10.1016/0092-8674(92)90093-R.

Volf, Miroslav. *A Public Faith: How Followers of Christ Should Serve the Common Good*. Brazos Press, 2011.

Walsh, James P. "Holy Time and Sacred Space in Puritan New England." *American Quarterly* 32, no. 1 (1980): 79–95. https://doi.org/10.2307/2712497.

Zimbardo, P. *The Lucifer Effect: Understanding How Good People Turn Evil*. Random House Publishing Group, 2008. https://books.google.com/books?id=vjeHCA6i4IAC.

ACKNOWLEDGMENTS

Thanks to Dr. Jim Carter and the team at PRCC for inviting me to be a part of this adventure. I send a special word of thanks to the constant encouragement of Dr. Michael Stewart, one of the top subject matter experts in healthcare chaplaincy in North America. I remember being a part of receiving Michael into the PCA a number of decades back. I saw an incredibly gifted individual on that day. He went even further than I could imagine. That fact has created a wealth of souls saved and lives transformed. For that, we all praise the Lord. Thanks, Michael. I express my gratitude to Dr. Rebecca Rine, one of the Church's most remarkable and gifted scholars who happens to serve with me as a research and project assistant. Thanks, Rebecca.

I want to also thank my wife, Mae, for

her loving support and our son, John Michael, for *being there*.

ABOUT THE AUTHOR

Michael A. Milton, Ph.D. is a Presbyterian minister (PCA), author and president of Faith for Living and the D. James Kennedy Institute of Reformed Leadership. The former chancellor-president of RTS, senior officer of Erskine Seminary, and a tenured professor, Mike is also a Chaplain (Colonel) US Army Retired. He founded and pastored churches in Kansas, Georgia, and North Carolina. He is the former pastor of the First Presbyterian Church of Chattanooga.

A graduate of UNC-Chapel Hill, among other associations, he cheers for the Tarheel and resides with Mae in the mountains of Western North Carolina. Learn more at https://michaelmilton.org/about. He writes regularly on Substack and for Carolina Journal, Christianity.com, Crosswalk.com, and WesternJournal.com.

ABOUT THE PRCC

The Presbyterian and Reformed Commission on Chaplains and Military Personnel

The Presbyterian and Reformed Commission on Chaplains and Military Personnel is a ministry of member denominations dedicated to obeying Christ's Great Commission by providing men to serve as chaplains in military and civilian organizations. The Commission endorses and ecclesiastically supports ordained, qualified chaplains; approves chaplain candidates; and helps presbyteries and congregations in biblical ministry to military personnel and their families.

The Rev. Dr. James Carter, Chaplain (LTC) US Army Retired, Executive Coordinator, PRCC and PCA Chaplain Ministries

The Chaplain Ministries Team

- Email: chaplainministries@pcanet.org
- Phone: 678-825-1251
- Gifts via check / money order made payable to MNA should be mailed to:
- Mission to North America
- P.O. Box 890233
- Charlotte, NC 28289-0233
- Learn more: https://pcamna.org/ministry/chaplain-ministries/

Michael A. Milton's *Involved with Mankind: A Theology of the Chaplaincy* is the first release in a series on the theology of chaplain ministry by the Presbyterian and Reformed Commission on Chaplains and Military Personnel (PRCC). Chaplain ministry is growing even as many churches are in decline. Why so? And how is it that chaplaincy seems to thrive in the secular age? How about the validity of a word and sacrament ministry that takes place in a context "outside of the gates" and is even funded by those who may be resistant to the Gospel? Mike Milton seeks to find not only the answers to these questions but to locate the theological code that can unlock the glorious potential of chaplaincy to be the faithful presence and common good that the Church seeks to become in secularism and post-secularism.

"Mike Milton thinks like a scholar but writes like a pastor. He takes subtle issues and, without dumbing them down, explains them in easy-to-understand terms. That is a wonderful gift to the Church."
—Joel Belz, Publisher, World Magazine

Dr. Michael Milton is one of the church's most outstanding and committed Christian leaders. He is a man of scholarship, intellect, and insight deeply devoted to the church of the Lord Jesus Christ. I am thankful for his contributions to evangelical thought and the life of our churches. We should all be thankful that his writings are available to evangelical Christians today."
—Dr. Albert Mohler, President, Southern Baptist Theological Seminary

Michael A. Milton (Ph.D., Wales) is a Presbyterian minister (PCA) and the Distinguished Professor of Missions and Evangelism at Erskine Theological Seminar. A founding pastor of three churches, and senior minister of a large historic downtown church, Dr. Milton was the fourth Chancellor-President of RTS. Milton is a Chaplain (Colonel) US Army, retired. He is also President of Faith for Living, Inc., a nonprofit ministry. Milton holds advanced degrees from UNC-Chapel Hill, Knox Seminary, and Erskine Seminary. He earned postdoctoral certification in Higher Education Teaching from Harvard. Mike and Mae Milton make their home in the Blue Ridge mountains of North Carolina.

www.ingramcontent.com/pod-product-compliance
Lightning Source LLC
Chambersburg PA
CBHW051234160726
47994CB00002B/874